L I G H T H O U S E S

LIGHT

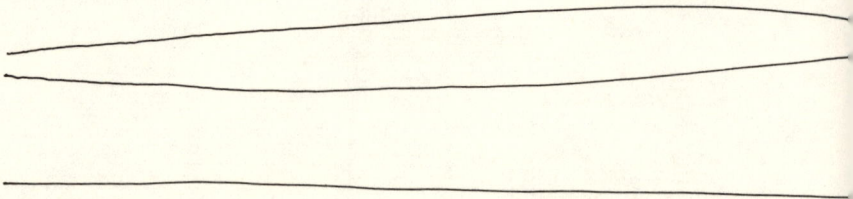

WRITTEN & ILLUSTRATED

HOUSES

The Light at Montauk Point, Long Island, New York

BY PAUL GIAMBARBA

The Scrimshaw Press
Centerville, Cape Cod, MA 02632-0010

Books by Paul Giambarba
Lighthouses
Blue Water Tales of Cape Cod
Cape Cod Fact and Folklore
Cape Cod Seashore Life
Whales, Whaling and Whalecraft
Surfmen and Lifesavers
Early Explorers of America
Going Whaling with Cap'n Goody
Around Cape Cod with Cap'n Goody
What is it at the Beach?
The Lighthouse at Dangerfield
Atlantic/Little, Brown

For a complete catalog of Scrimshaw Press books,
send a self-addressed stamped envelope with your request to:
The Scrimshaw Press
P. O. Box 10
Centerville, MA 02632-0010

Printed in the United States of America
ISBN 0-87155-122-5

Second Printing

Roman Light at Ostia, 50 A.D.

As long as there have been ships, there has been a need for lighthouses.

The ocean is often dangerous.
Howling winds and mountainous seas
can carry a vessel up on a sand bar
miles from shore
and break it to bits.

Waves can smash a ship
against a rocky coast.

Lighthouses were built
to warn sailors to keep away
from sand bars and rocks.
Sailors see the light and have time
to steer away from danger.

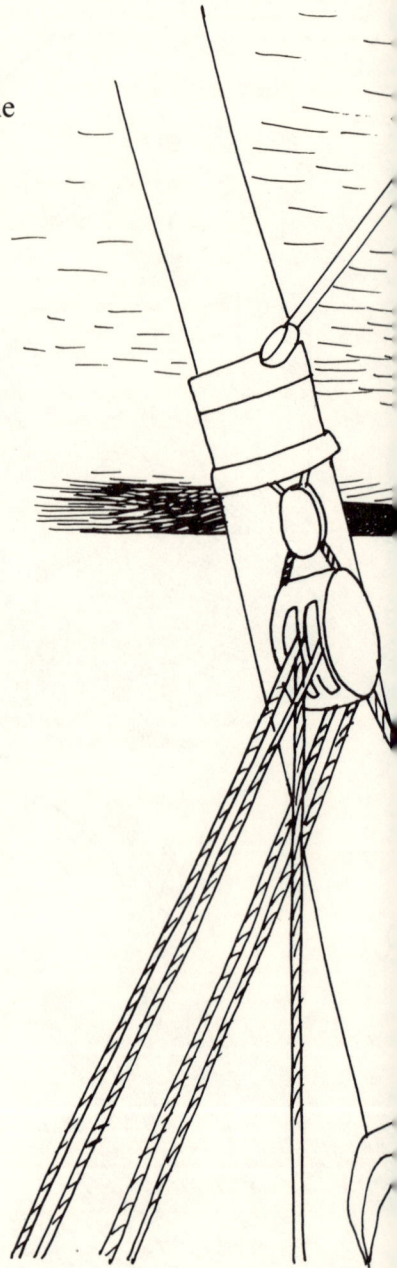

The first warning lights were simply
huge fires burned every night
on the coast.

Or they were landmarks such as
volcanos whose smoldering glow
could be seen at night.

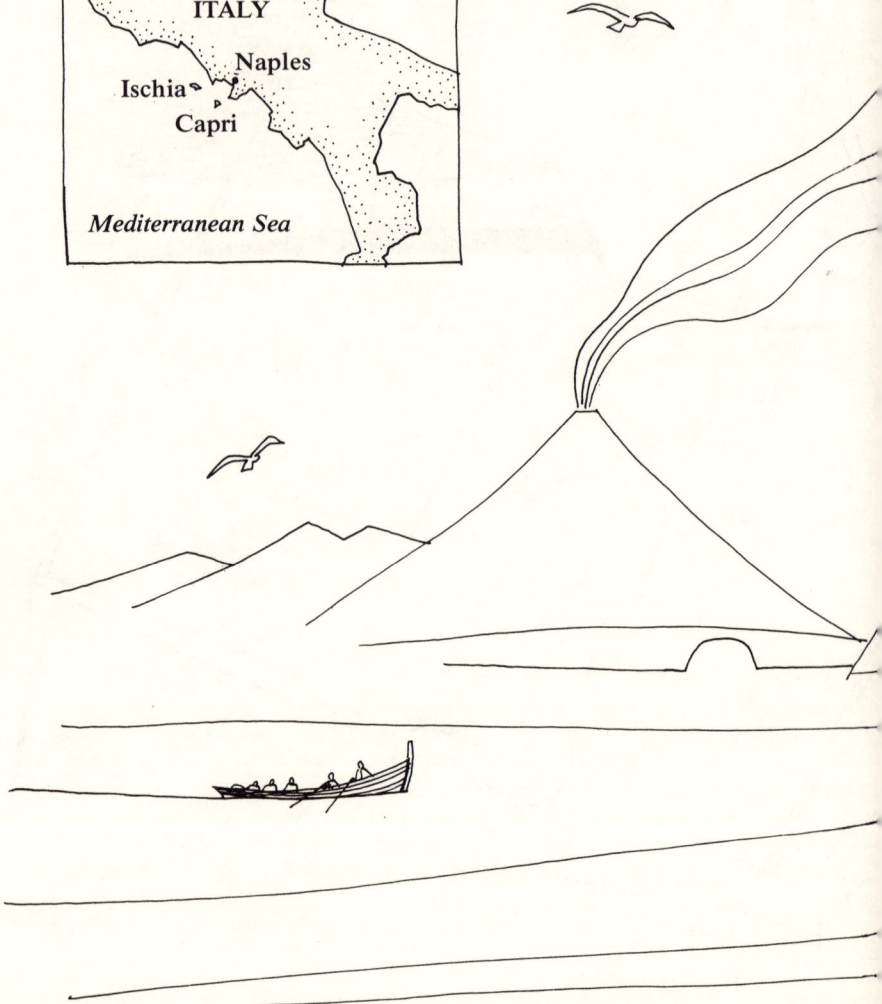

Rome

ITALY

Naples

Ischia

Capri

Mediterranean Sea

Mount Vesuvius, Naples, Italy, and the castle of Ischia.

The first lighthouses were among
the great wonders of the ancient world:
the Pharos at Alexandria, in Egypt;
the Colossus at Rhodes,
an island in the Mediterranean
off the coast of Greece.

Both were built about 300 years
before the birth of Christ.

GREECE

TURKEY

Rhodes

Cyprus

Crete

Mediterranean Sea

Jerusalem

Alexandria

EGYPT

Nile River

Pharos at Alexandria, Egypt.

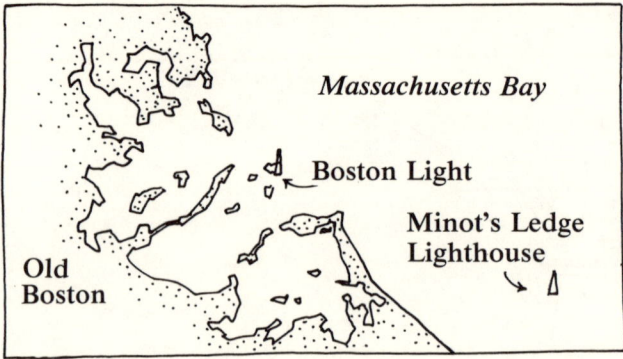

Massachusetts Bay

Boston Light

Minot's Ledge
Lighthouse

Old
Boston

The first lighthouse built in North America was Boston Light, established in 1716, on Little Brewster Island in Boston Harbor.

Boston Light, from a print of 1729.
An English sloop-of-war rests at anchor in the foreground.

By 1800, lighthouses had been built along the Atlantic coast from St. John's, Newfoundland to Tybee, Georgia.

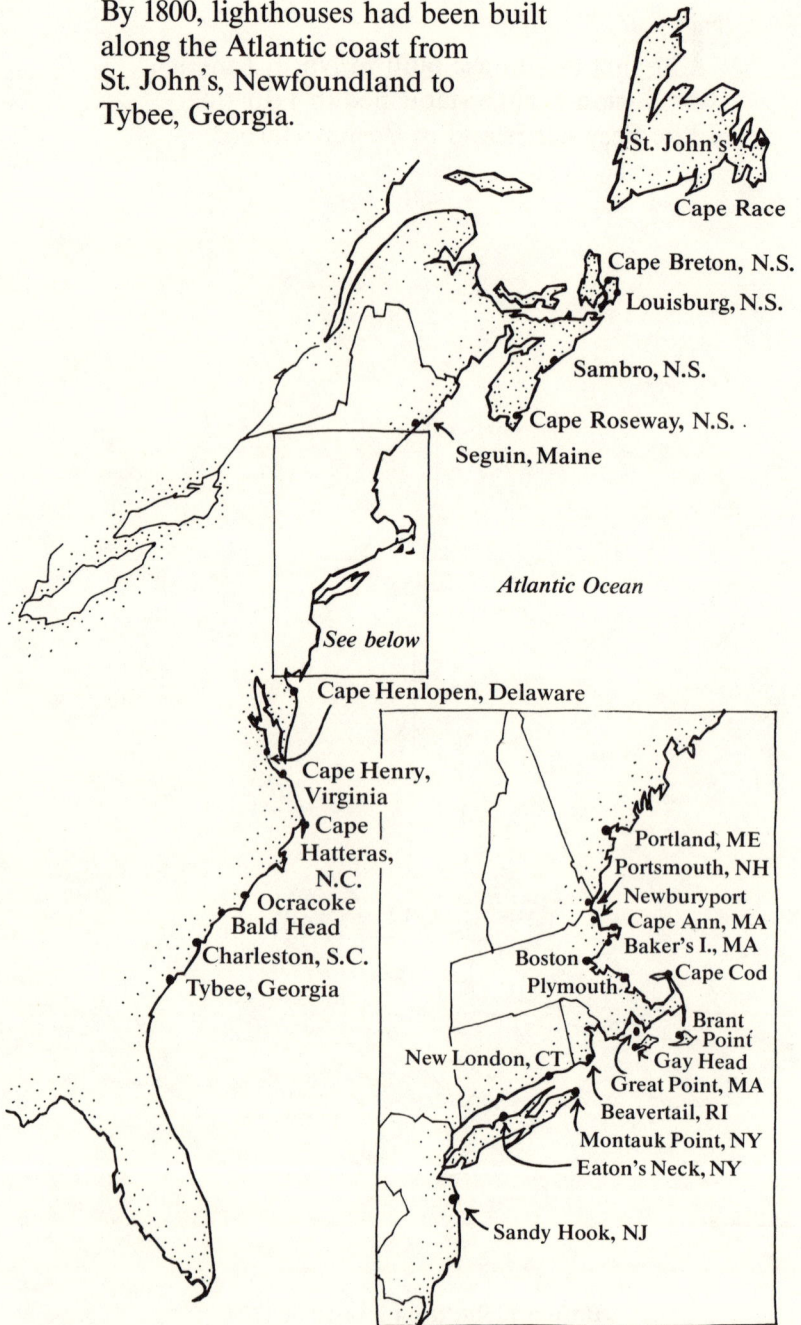

St. John's

Cape Race

Cape Breton, N.S.

Louisburg, N.S.

Sambro, N.S.

Cape Roseway, N.S.

Seguin, Maine

Atlantic Ocean

See below

Cape Henlopen, Delaware

Cape Henry, Virginia

Cape Hatteras, N.C.

Ocracoke

Bald Head

Charleston, S.C.

Tybee, Georgia

Portland, ME

Portsmouth, NH

Newburyport

Cape Ann, MA

Baker's I., MA

Boston

Cape Cod

Plymouth

Brant Point

Gay Head

New London, CT

Great Point, MA

Beavertail, RI

Montauk Point, NY

Eaton's Neck, NY

Sandy Hook, NJ

Cape Race, Newfoundland

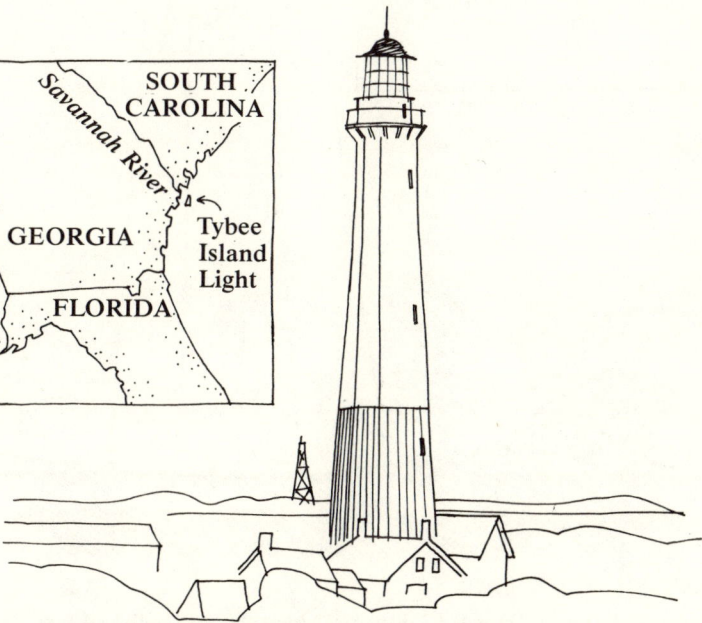

SOUTH CAROLINA

Savannah River

GEORGIA

Tybee Island Light

FLORIDA

Tybee Island Light, Georgia.

Lighthouses can be seen at some
of the same places today:
Sandy Hook, New Jersey, and
North Truro, on Cape Cod,
Massachusetts.

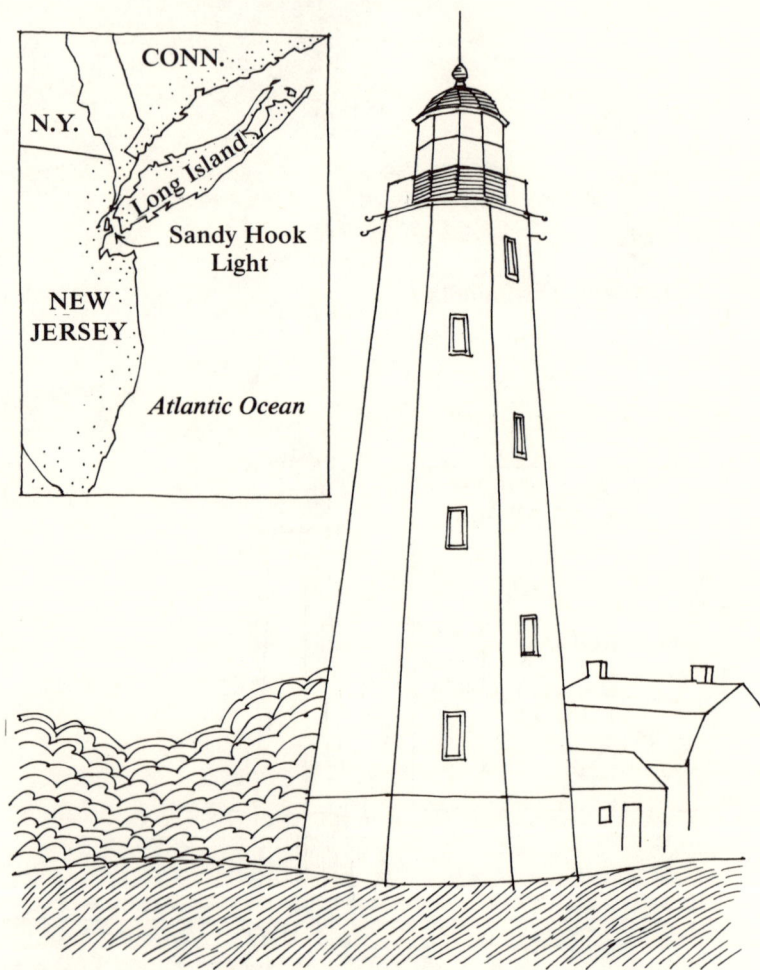

CONN.

N.Y.

Long Island

Sandy Hook
Light

NEW
JERSEY

Atlantic Ocean

**Sandy Hook Lighthouse, New Jersey, is the oldest
standing lighthouse in the United States, dating from 1764.**

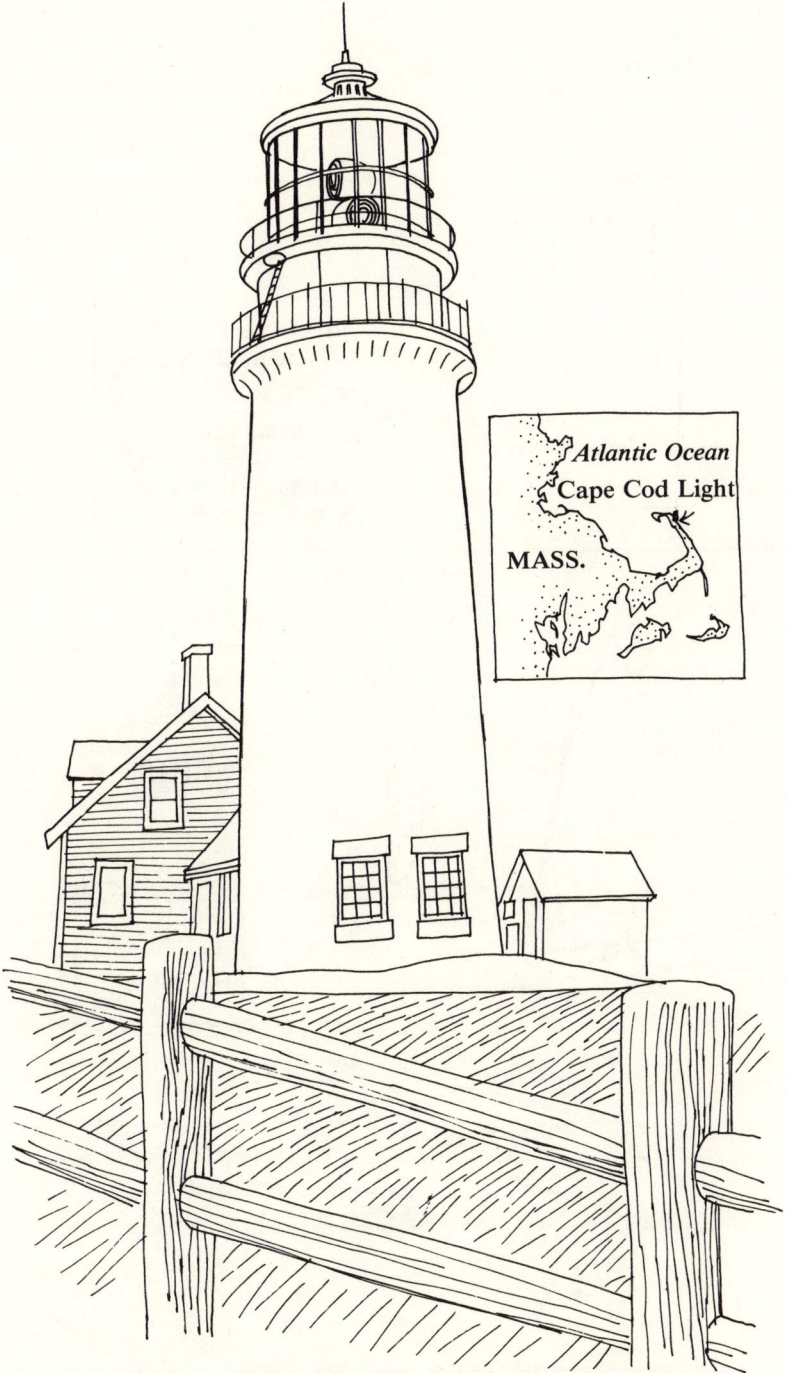

Atlantic Ocean
Cape Cod Light
MASS.

Cape Cod Light, North Truro, MA, 1797. Rebuilt 1851.

Brant Point, Nantucket;

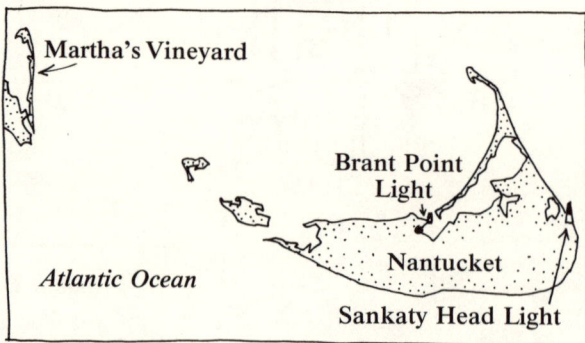

Catboats rounding Brant Point, Nantucket, about 1900.

Gay Head, Martha's Vineyard,
both in Massachusetts;

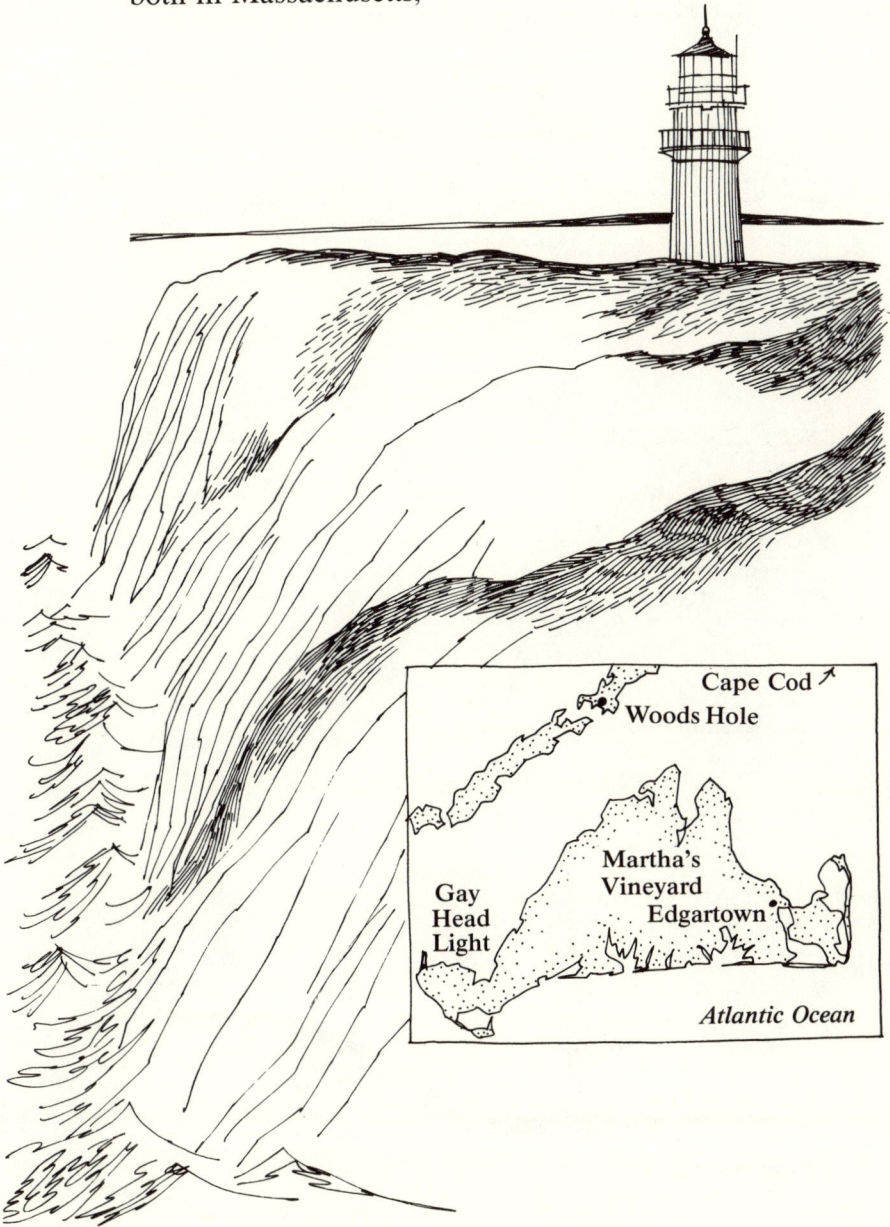

Gay Head Cliffs, Martha's Vineyard, MA.

Montauk Point, Long Island, New York;
Cape Henry, Virginia;

Montauk Point, Long Island.

New and old lighthouses at Cape Henry, Virginia,
built in 1881 (left) and 1792 (right).

and Cape Hatteras, North Carolina.
This lighthouse tower is striped black and white
in the spiral pattern of a candy cane.

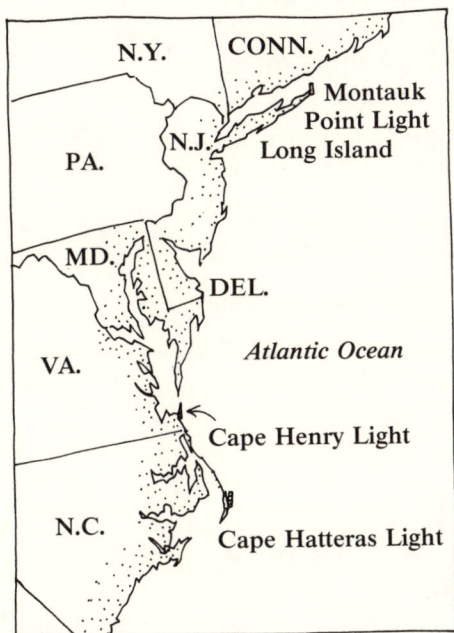

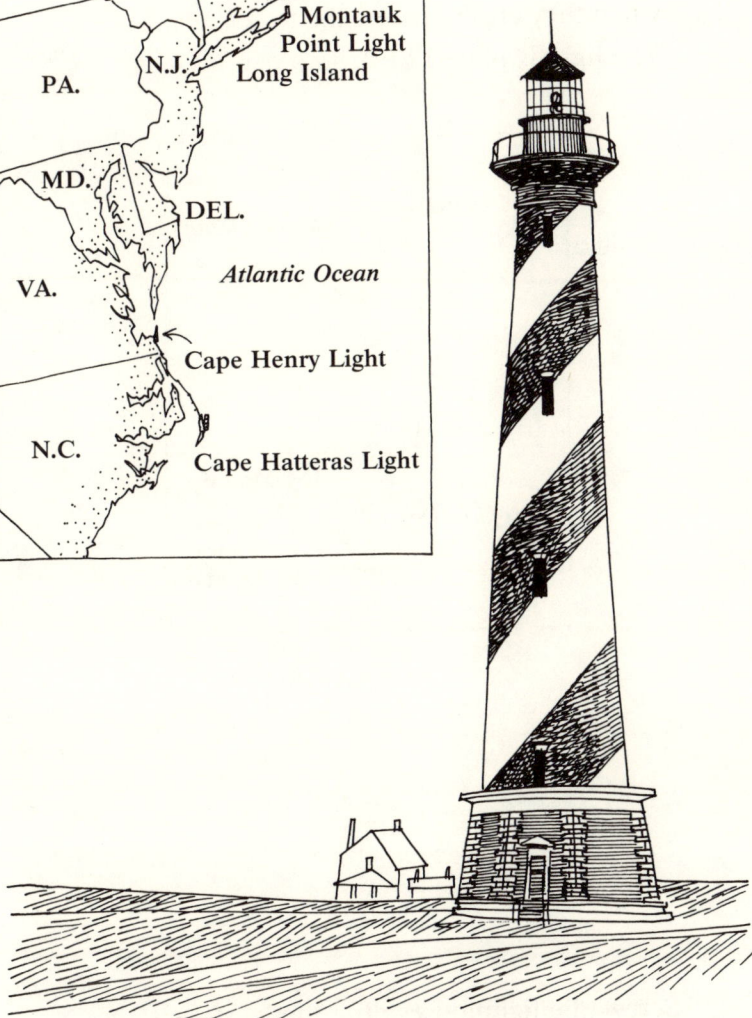

Cape Hatteras, North Carolina.
This is the tallest lighthouse tower in the United States,
200 feet from the base to the lantern.

Lighthouses are towers.
A few have square sides, but most are round
to better resist the wind and waves.
The sides often curve to a narrow top so that
heavy seas will fall back upon themselves
when they crash against the tower.

The light is placed high, so it can be seen.

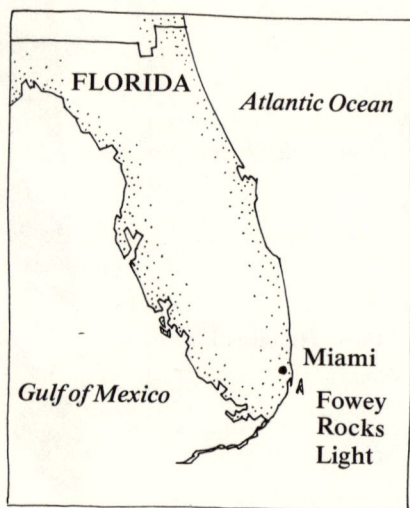

Screw pile lighthouses offer the least resistance
to waves. Heavy seas can crash through the open
framework. The piles or steel rods are driven, or
screwed, into the ocean floor.

Fowey Rocks Light, eleven miles southeast of Miami,
built in 1878.

The first lighthouses used candles
for their lamps. Then, whale oil lamps were used.
When whales became scarce and whale oil costly,
other oils were tried.
1n 1878 kerosene came into use.

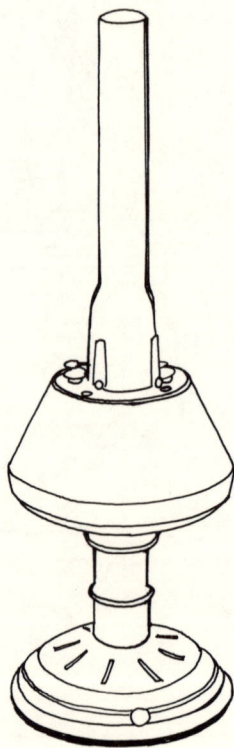

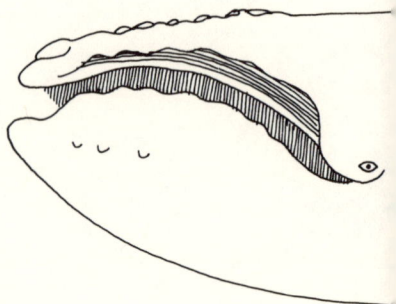

Whale oil lighthouse lantern, 19th century.

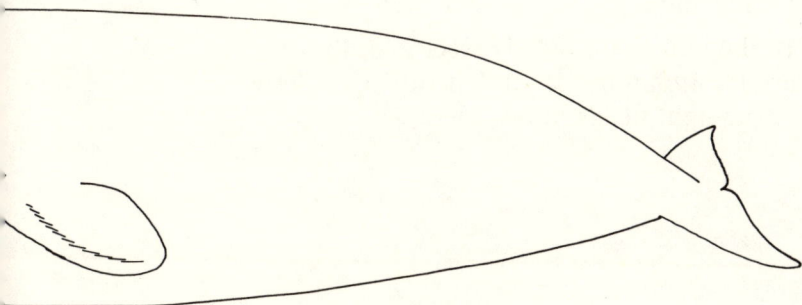

North Atlantic Right Whale

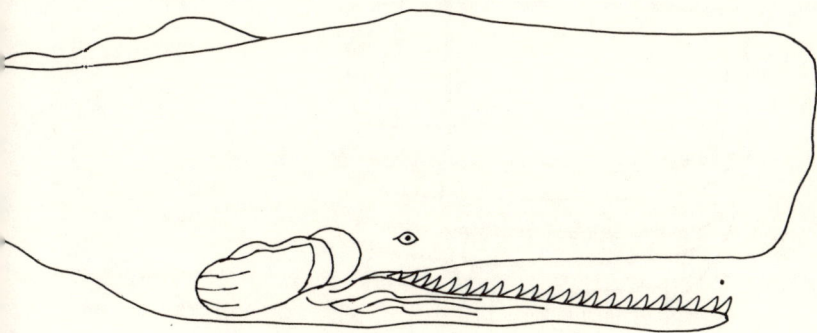

Sperm Whale

Whale oil was made by "trying out" or cooking
the blubber of these whales.

The light of the oil lamps was magnified and projected by glass lenses. These were made of polished glass in many different shapes and sizes.

Some lenses were as wide as eight-and-one-half feet or more across the middle and ten to fifteen feet in height. Some carried the light of the lamps for 20 miles or more.

Today, the lamps are mostly electric bulbs or powerful searchlights. It all depends upon how strong the light needs to be.

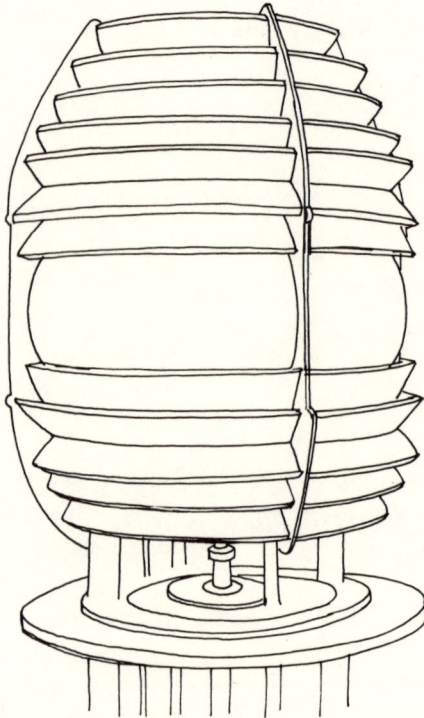

A 19th century lighthouse lens.

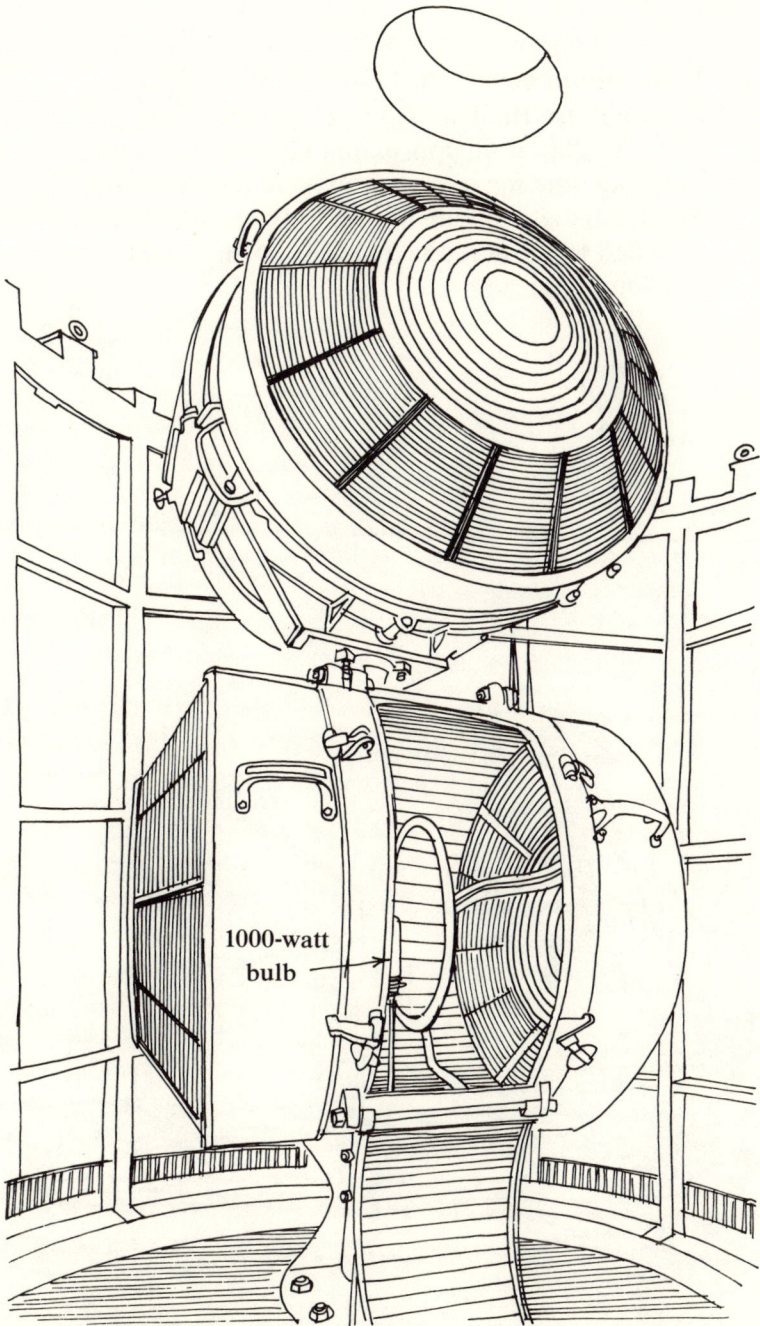

Electric beacons at Cape Cod Light, North Truro, MA.

Each station usually has a different signal from its neighbors. In this way vessels caught in fog can tell from the sound approximately where they are. Years ago the fog signals were sounded by hand. Small engines were then used until electricity was supplied to the stations. Now, most fog signals are automatic.

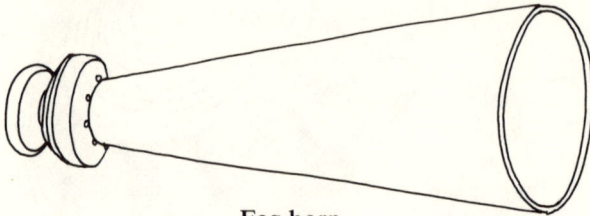

Fog horn

bell

Old light at Hallett's Point, East River (Hell Gate), NY.

Each lighthouse station also maintains some sort of fog signal. In thick fog even the most powerful light is of little use. Sound signals can be heard for many miles across the water. Guns, bells, horns, sirens and whistles have all been tried with success. Boston Light had a fog gun for signalling as early as 1719.

Fog gun at Boston Light, 1900.

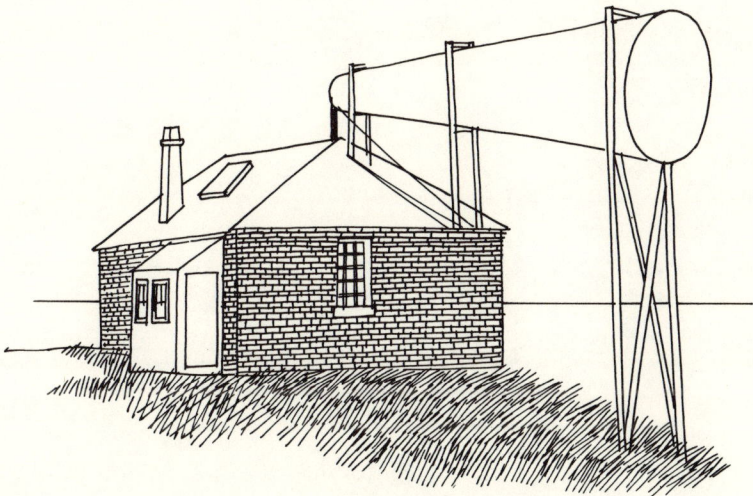

Siren at Baker's Island, MA

The whole top of a lighthouse is a giant lantern. It is reached after many turns around a curving staircase. Windows are set into the thick walls of the towers to light the stairway during the day.

The machine that moved the lenses around the lamp was called the "clock." Years ago, this clock had to be wound by hand every few hours.

Nowadays many lights are automatic.
Even in the worst storm the light comes on at dusk and casts its beam without fail.

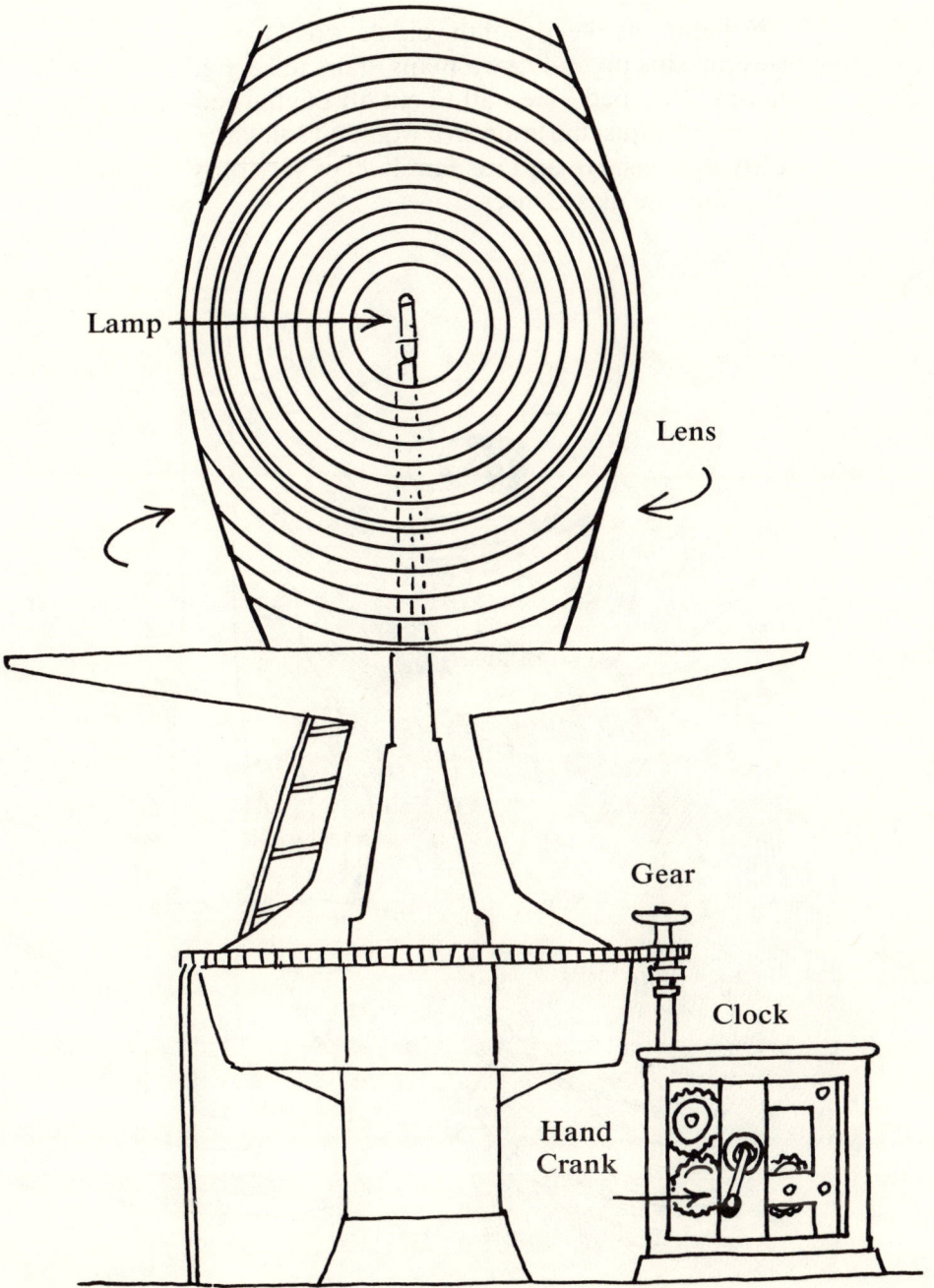

Lamp

Lens

Gear

Clock

Hand
Crank

The lighthouse keeper of the old days had to make several trips up and down many stairs to keep his lamps "trimmed." He had to cut off the burned wick and adjust the lamp so it wouldn't smoke and dirty the lens. He and his family kept very busy cleaning the glass lenses.

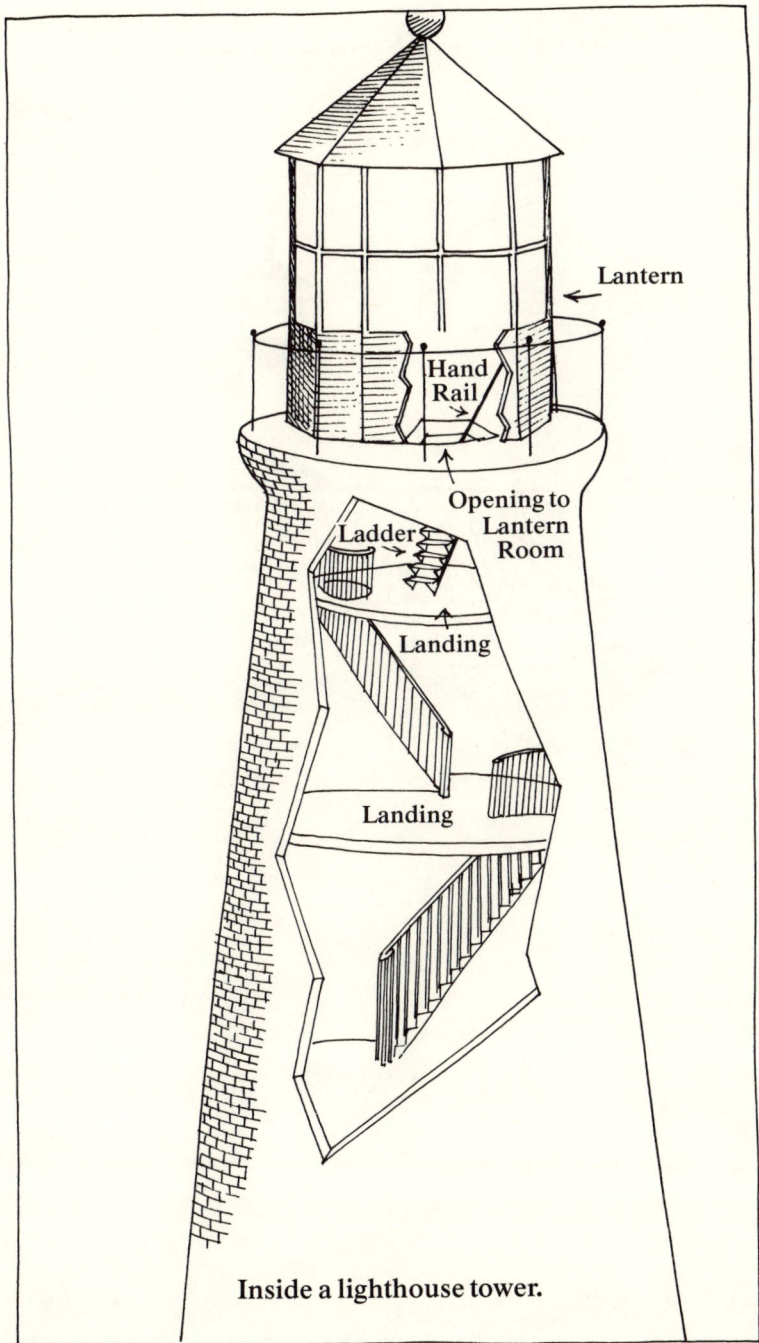

Lantern

Hand Rail

Opening to Lantern Room

Ladder

Landing

Landing

Inside a lighthouse tower.

Sankaty Head Light, Nantucket, Massachusetts

In spite of seemingly endless chores,
living at a lighthouse was often exciting.

The keeper's house was usually built of wood and
attached to the base of the tower.
During great storms danger was always present.

Abbie Burgess was only fourteen when her father became keeper of the twin Matinicus Rock Lights, 22 miles out in Penobscot Bay on the Maine Coast, in the year 1853. When Sam Burgess went to the mainland for supplies, she took care of the lights.

The great winter storm of January 19, 1856 struck Matinicus Rock when Sam was away. On the rock Abby cared for her three younger sisters and her sick mother, besides tending the twin lights.
For four weeks the angry seas prevented Keeper Burgess from returning home, but Abbie kept the lights burning. When mountainous waves destroyed the Burgess home and all the other wooden buildings on the rock, Abbie moved her family to safety in the tower of one of the lights.

Lighthouses, Matinicus Island, Maine.

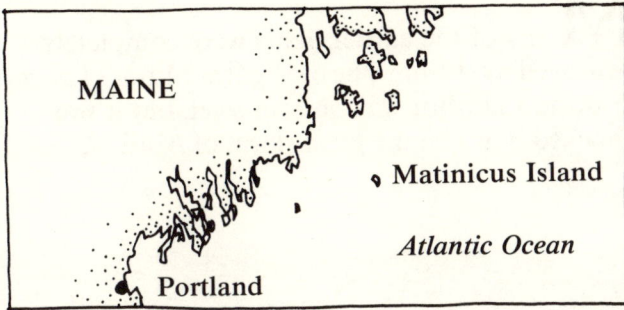

Another severe storm the following year kept Sam Burgess away from home once more, this time for 21 days. He had gone to the mainland for his pay and supplies of food. Again, Abbie kept the lights going without fail, though her rations were down to one egg and a cup of cornmeal a day.

Many of the earlier lights were completely destroyed by storms. The old light at Minot's Ledge in Boston Harbor was built of steel, but it was knocked down in the great storm of April 17, 1851.

The present light was built in 1860 of granite blocks carved into the ledge and put together like pieces of a giant jigsaw puzzle. No storm has wrecked it, but furious seas have tried to do so many times.

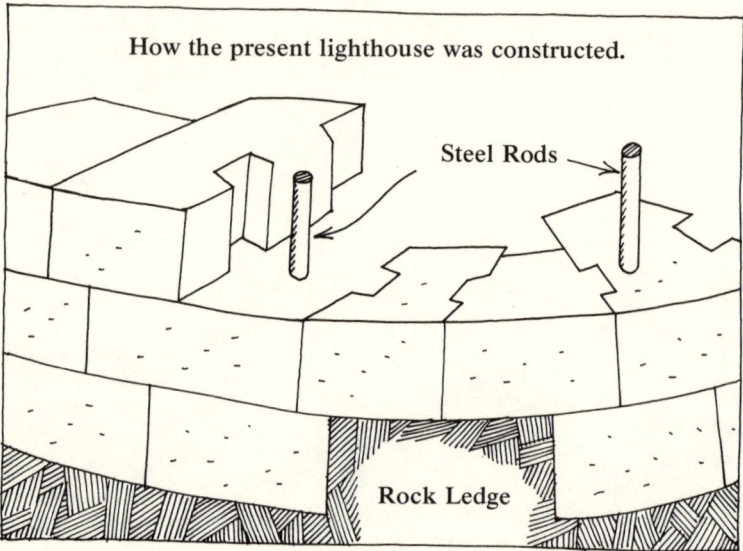

How the present lighthouse was constructed.

Steel Rods

Rock Ledge

E ach light has its own signal.
Some don't move; these are called "fixed" lights.
Some have more than one lamp.
Some move in a circle.

In the old days, the prisms of the lenses
moving around the lamp shaped the light
of the lamp into beams, or flashes.
Today the flashing is done by electricity
and the moving lens isn't needed.

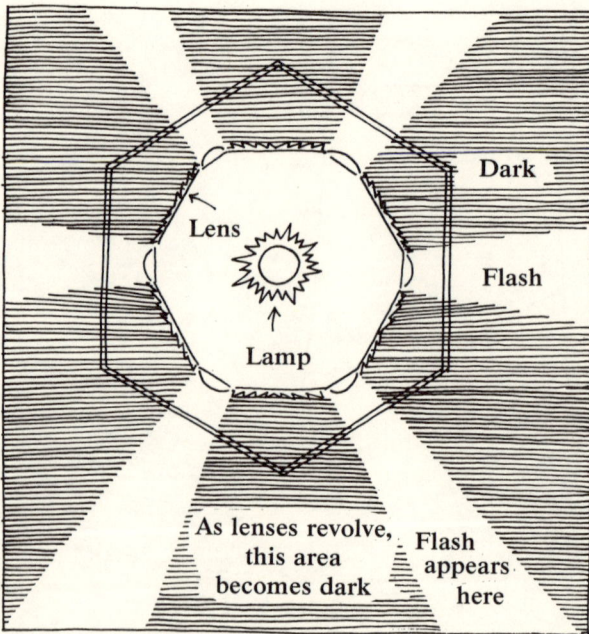

Dark

Lens

Flash

Lamp

As lenses revolve,
this area
becomes dark

Flash
appears
here

Bird's eye view of a simple flashing light.

Portland Head Light, Portland, Maine,
is a flashing light, the first beacon erected
by the United States on January 10, 1791.

Flashing lights are generally used
for more exposed positions
than fixed lights.

Grindle Point Light, Isleboro, Maine,
is a fixed light on Long Island
in Penobscot Bay.

By flashing, a light has its own pattern, or code.
The light on Minot's Ledge in Boston Harbor
had the nicest flash of all - ---- ---, 1-4-3,
or: flash, stop; flash, flash, flash, flash, stop:
flash, flash, flash.
Some say it stands for I LOVE YOU.

ABOUT THE AUTHOR

PAUL GIAMBARBA began his career as a copy boy with the *Boston Post*. He was also a sports cartoonist for the *Boston Herald*, a contributor to *True, Sports Illustrated*, and a weekly contributor to *This Week* and two *Scholastic Magazines*. In 1965 he began The Scrimshaw Press to make available abundantly illustrated original material in paperback form at modest prices. Books from The Scrimshaw Press have been reviewed by *Scientific American, The Boston Globe, American Artist, National Fisherman, Library Journal, School Library Journal, Horn Book* and *Scholastic Teacher*. Articles about The Scrimshaw Press have appeared in *American Artist* and *Horn Book*. In 1969 Atlantic/Little, Brown published Paul Giambarba's *The Lighthouse at Dangerfield*, a book about Highland Light on Cape Cod.

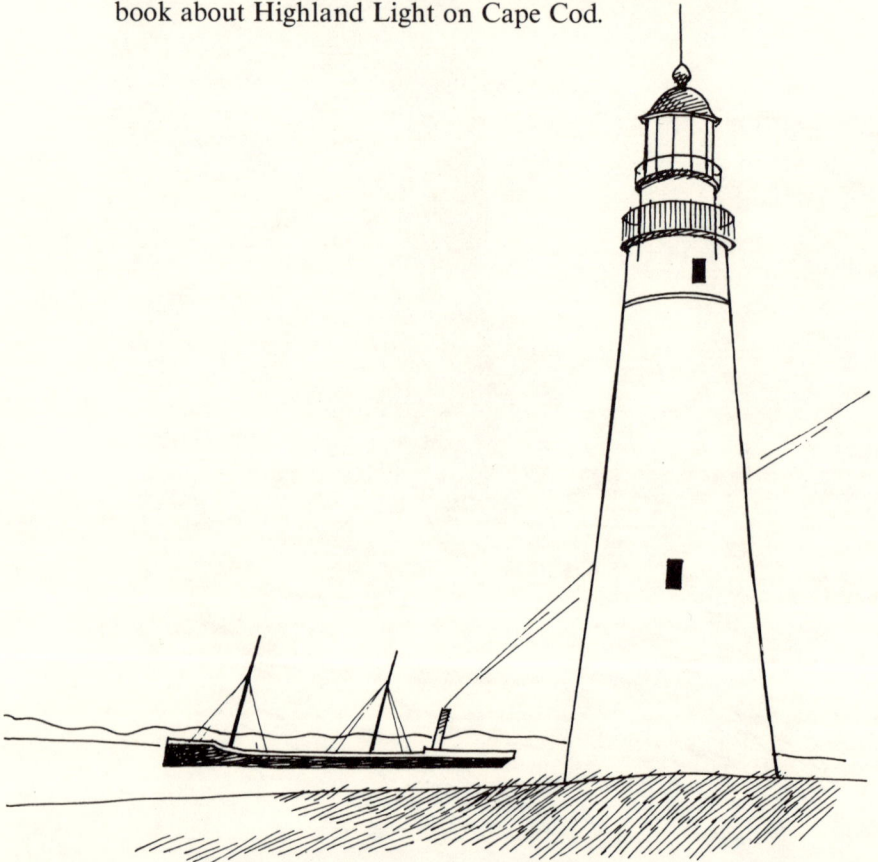

Fort Gratiot Light on Lake Huron.
The original tower of 1825 was rebuilt in 1861.